D1495434

DISCARD

BC
201367

CUSTOMS · COSTUMES AND CULTURES

MASKS

by
Kevin K. Casey

Rourke Publications, Inc.
Vero Beach, Florida 32964

PHOTO CREDITS

© Photophile, L.L.T. Rhodes: page 5; © Jerry Craven: pages 7, 14, 15, 16, 17, 21; © Photophile: pages 9, 10; © Picture Library Associates, Milt Haertig: pages 11, 30; © Kevin K. Casey: pages 12, 13; © Photophile, Glasheen Graphics: pages 19, 23; © Picture Library Associates, Carol Hayman: page 24; © Photophile, Jose Carrillo: page 25; © Photophile, Alan C. Craft: page 26; © Picture Library Associates, Kurt Vail: page 27; © Picture Library Associates, Mary Goodspeed: page 28; © Photophile, Orin Cassill: page 29

ACKNOWLEDGEMENTS

I am grateful to Jerry Craven and Ann Sloan for their generous assistance in producing the photographs that appear in chapters 2, 5, 6, and 7.

I also wish to thank Photophile of San Diego, California, and Picture Library Associates of Guadalupe, California, for providing the other color photographs of masks throughout the world.

Library of Congress Cataloging-in-Publication Data

Casey, Kevin, 1967-
      Masks / by Kevin K. Casey.
          p.   cm. — (Customs, costumes and cultures)
      Includes index.
      Summary: explains that throughout history people all over the world have used masks for religious purposes as well as for disguise, protection, and enjoyment.
      ISBN 0-86625-592-3
      1. Masks—Social aspects—Juvenile literature. 2. Masks—Religious aspects—Juvenile literature. [1. Masks.] I. Title. II. Series.
GT1747.C37   1996
391'.434—dc20   96-11394
                                                                                    CIP
                                                                                    AC

Printed in the U.S.A.

TABLE OF CONTENTS

CHAPTER 1
Prehistoric Masks

People have worn masks for a long time. Since before written history, people wore masks. Sometimes they wore masks for religious reasons. Sometimes they wore masks to perform magic. Other times they wore masks just for fun.

In a cave in southwestern France called the Trois Frere, there are Stone Age paintings of men wearing masks in the shapes of animal heads. **Anthropologists** (an thruh PAH luh jists) believe that these paintings show hunters stalking prey or performing a hunting dance. In South Africa there are similar rock paintings of men in masks.

TOO BIG TO WEAR

Some people value their masks so much that they do not wear them. The Dogon tribe of Mali, in Africa, have huge masks over 30 feet long. The Dogon do not wear these masks because they are too big and valuable. Instead the Dogon keep the large masks in special places so members of the tribe can admire them.

These men of the Chimbu tribe in New Guinea dance in the costumes and masks they wear into battle. They believe the dance helps them win battles.

The first images of people wearing masks were of men hunting or preparing to hunt. Most early masks looked like animals. In a ritual called **pantomime magic** (PAN tuh miim MA jik), men performed ceremonies to help make the hunt successful. Some people believed that if a man pretended to shoot another man who was wearing the mask or head of an animal, the hunter would be successful in the real hunt.

Another reason people wore animal masks was to get the power of the animal. Since prehistoric times, people all over the world have believed in the magical power of masks. Some thought masks had the power to change people into powerful warriors, fearsome beasts, and even spirits.

CHAPTER 2
Metal and Stone Masks

People of many cultures have used masks to cover the faces of the dead. Unlike the wooden masks that living people wore, death masks were usually made of metal or stone. The ancient Egyptians believed that the ghosts of dead people would return to their bodies. To make sure that the bodies were in good condition when the ghosts returned, the Egyptians mummified the bodies. They made gold masks in the shape of the dead person's face. The gold mask helped the ghost recognize its body.

The Egyptians were not the only people to make masks for the dead. Seventeen hundred years ago, in the area of Mexico that is now Mexico City, the Teotihuacan people made masks of stone for their dead. The Teotihuacans believed that they might escape death if they honored those who had died. Other tribes in the same area of Mexico made masks of turquoise for their dead.

Funerals were only one reason that ancient people made masks. Thousands of years before movies or television, the ancient Greeks enjoyed watching plays. These plays were performed in large outdoor arenas called **amphitheaters** (AM fuh thee uh turz). The actors in the plays often wore masks to show whether their characters were happy or sad. The ancient Greeks used masks for entertainment, something we still do today.

Like the ancient Greeks, many people still use masks during plays or ceremonies. This mask is from the Indonesian island of Bali.

CHAPTER 3
Animal Heritage

Masks are an important part of life for Natives Americans. Along the Pacific coast, from northern California to southern Alaska, many tribes use masks to celebrate their heritage and religion. Most Native American masks in this region are made of wood. Tribes like the Kwakiutl, Nootka, Tlingit, and Haida use masks in ceremonies that tell stories about their past.

One legend describes how a tribal ancestor lived in the home of an animal. He stayed with the animal for a long time. After he learned many things from the animal, he returned to the world of people and started a tribe. Ever since, the tribe retells the story through a ceremony with dancers who wear animal masks.

Another belief many tribes have is that spirits visit them during the winter. At this time, the tribes perform masked dances. They believe that spirits communicate with some members of the tribe. When members receive a message from a spirit, they must tell the rest of the tribe the message. They do this by performing a dance and song at a tribal meeting called a **tamanawas.** During the performance the dancers wear masks in the shape of the spirit that has spoken to them.

NOT ALL MASKS ARE FOR HEADS

Most people wear masks on their faces, but some people wear masks on other places. The Alaskan Eskimos make little masks, called "finger masks." The Eskimos wear these masks on their fingers during special celebrations.

Some people wear masks on their clothes. Leaders in some tribes in Siberia make masks and attach them to their robes.

Native American tribes living along the northwest Pacific coast of North America make colorful and fierce looking wooden masks.

CHAPTER 4
Totem Poles

To many people, masks are more than wood carvings. Masks are important tools for religious ritual. Some cultures have important rules about how to take care of masks. Native Americans of the northwest Pacific coast have many different rules, for different kinds of masks. They use some masks only once and then burn them. They keep others for four years. They hide some masks in the forest, and they give other masks away as gifts. Many families hand down masks from generation to generation.

Native Americans carved this totem pole near Ketchican, Alaska.

This giant totem pole stands on an island off the coast of western Canada.

In addition to masks for people to wear, the Native Americans of the northwest Pacific coast make huge poles with faces carved onto them. These poles are called **totem poles** (TOH tum POHLZ). Totem poles are often as large as trees. Some faces are animals, like birds. All of the faces are painted in bright colors.

The animal faces on a totem pole honor the animals that protect the tribe. The people of the tribe always show respect to the animal on their totem poles. Since the animal protects the tribe, killing the animal, even for food, is forbidden. Any member of the tribe that harms the animal is punished, maybe even killed.

CHAPTER 5
Hundreds of Little Gods

The Pueblo Indians of Arizona and New Mexico have kept many of their traditions from before the time of the Spanish invaders, called conquistadors. Because the southwest Native American tribes live in desert regions, rain is important to them. People need rain to grow crops and for drinking water. Pueblo Indians perform many ceremonies to help produce rain.

The Hopi and Zuni tribes believe in hundreds of little gods called **kachinas** (kuh CHEE nuhz). According to legend, the kachinas first brought water and the knowledge of how to plant corn to the Pueblo Indians. When the kachinas moved to the bottom of a desert lake, they left masks behind. The kachinas left the masks so that they could return to the Pueblo Indians.

Kachinas are happy gods who love to dance. Throughout the year, Pueblo Indians perform many dances while wearing kachina masks. Kachina masks are usually large masks made of wood, rawhide, and gourds. Some are decorated with fur, feathers, and paint.

Legend says that it was the kachinas who taught the Hopi and Zuni tribes to plant corn.

The Hopi and Zuni believe that masks help kachinas return to the tribes.

Every winter Pueblo Indians perform their largest ceremony, the **shalako** (SHAL ah ko). Before the dancers perform the ceremony in public, they practice in an underground meeting place called a **kiva** (KEE vuh). The dancers pay close attention to the masks and costumes. If even one feather is out of place, the magic may not work.

In addition to performing dances while wearing kachina masks, the Hopi and Zuni tribes also make small dolls in honor of their many gods.

13

CHAPTER 6
Spirits and Ancestors

Masks are important to the people of Africa. Africans use masks in ceremonies of many kinds. Like the Native Americans of the Pacific Northwest, some Africans believe in the power of

animal spirits. Some tribes believe that certain animals are their guardians. By performing a dance while wearing an animal mask made of wood, the tribe shows respect to the animal spirit. If the spirit is pleased, it will continue protecting the tribe.

Many African tribes use masks in ceremonies to honor their ancestors.

Africans also wear masks to honor spirits of people. Some African tribes believe that the spirits of their dead ancestors stay with the tribe. These Africans welcome their ancestors' spirits, who stay in the village along with the living members of the tribe. Since the spirits of the ancestors are always around, it is important be friendly to them. Tribesmen keep their ancestors happy by sometimes wearing masks and performing dances in honor of their dead friends and relatives.

Some African masks look like the faces of ancestors or spirits. Other masks do not look like the faces of dead relatives or friends, but they are still important in tribal rituals. Masks and other works of art that do not look like their subject are called *abstract*. African masks have been a major influence on modern abstract art.

Not all African masks look exactly like people or animals. African masks have been an important influence on modern abstract art.

CHAPTER 7
Life and Death

Africa is a large continent with many different groups of people. The masks of Africa, and the way tribes use them, are as different as the tribes of Africa. Some tribes use masks to celebrate life. Other tribes use masks for funerals, and some tribes use masks to celebrate both life and death.

African masks are used for many reasons, including the celebration of growing up and honoring dead relatives.

There are many different types of African masks. This one is decorated with jewelry made from small shells.

Some tribes in central Africa use masks to celebrate the change from boyhood to manhood. When a boy reaches the right age, he must perform a ritual before the other tribesmen will think of him as a man. First, the boy wears a mask that stands for his childhood. After a while, he throws off the mask. This shows the end of his childhood, and the boy changes into a young man. When the ceremony is over, the young man gets a smaller mask, and he wears it on a necklace. This small mask will bring the young man good luck.

Some Africans also wear masks during funerals. The Dogon tribe uses masks after a member of the tribe has died. In a six-day ceremony, tribesmen use masks to encourage the ghost of the dead tribesman to leave the village. The villagers wear large masks and perform many dances. After the last dance, the ghost leaves the village, and life returns to normal.

CHAPTER 8
The Shaman

Among Eskimo tribes living near the Bering Strait, a narrow body of water separating North America and Asia, there is an important member of the tribe called a **shaman** (SHAH mun). The shaman uses masks to help the tribe. Many tribes around the world have shamans. To the Eskimo people, the shaman is a wise person. The shaman uses his or her knowledge to make life easier for the tribe.

One way a shaman helps the tribe is by curing disease. Some Eskimos believe that angry spirits cause sickness. The spirits might become angry because someone has said or done something that is against tribal law. When that person becomes ill, the shaman wears a mask and performs a dance while speaking in a secret language. Only the shaman and the spirits know the secret language. Through the dance, the shaman hopes to make the spirits happy again. If the spirits are pleased, they may take away the sickness.

Another important duty of the shaman is to aid in hunting and fishing. By wearing masks and dancing, the shaman speaks with the spirits to help bring good hunting and good weather. Sometimes the shaman also discovers the best places to catch fish.

Many tribes around the world have a member, called a shaman, who uses masks in magical ceremonies.

CHAPTER 9
Masks in the South Seas

People living on the islands in the south Pacific Ocean often wear masks. Masks are important in the daily life of living people, and masks are important in funeral ceremonies for members of the tribe who have died.

Many tribes of the South Pacific believe in a special power called *mana*. Mana is a power that determines how well people live. Priests and chiefs have more mana than common men, but common men need mana, too. The common tribesmen try to get mana by honoring special spirits. For instance, a canoe builder uses masks and ceremonial dances to honor the spirit of canoe building. If the spirit is pleased, it will grant more mana to the canoe builder.

In New Guinea, natives prepare a special funeral when several tribesmen die. After a feast, masked dancers perform a ritual to attract the ghosts of the dead. After the dance is over, the dancers place the masks on a raft and push it into the middle of a river. The ghosts travel down the river with the raft and masks. When the raft reaches the mouth of the river and enters the sea, the chief of the tribe orders the ghosts to change into sharks and crocodiles.

Bumbun tribesmen in western Malaysia along the Straight of Malacca often wear masks during important rituals.

CHAPTER 10
The Mayordomo

The origin of masks in Mexico dates back thousands of years, long before the first conquistadors arrived. Most historians and anthropologists believe that masks were first used in the religious ceremonies of the Mexican Indians. In the feast of **Atamalqualiztli,** Aztec dancers dunked their heads into water barrels full of snakes and frogs. The dancers swallowed the snakes and frogs alive.

Today masks are still important in Mexican celebrations. All Mexican villages have celebrations called *fiestas.* Most fiestas have masked dancers. Dancers must train and practice the proper way to dance with the mask. Fiestas are a source of pride for the villages. The dancers must work hard to make sure their performance is perfect.

Since the fiestas are so important to Mexican villages, each village has a person in charge of the masks. This person is the *mayordomo.* The mayordomo is just as important to each village as the *alcalde,* or town mayor. The mayordomo is in charge of choosing the masked dancers, training them, storing the masks between fiestas, and providing food for the dancers during the fiesta. If the mayordomo and the masked dancers work well together, the fiesta will be a success and the whole village will be happy.

Mexican villagers take care of festival masks. In Mexican villages, the mayordomo cares for the masks and trains the dancers who wear the masks.

CHAPTER 11
Historic Battles

From the state of Sonora in northern Mexico to Chiapas along the Guatemalan border, Mexicans make and use masks in many fiestas and holidays.

In central Mexico, near Mexico City, local people act out the conquest of Mexico City by Cortez and his conquistadors. The ceremony has many masked dancers who represent the defenders of the city. There are also dancers who represent the conquistadors. The dance begins by showing the battle between the city and the conquistadors, and ends with the capture of Mexico City.

These Mexican Americans in Austin, Texas, wear masks during the el día de los muertos, *or Day of the Dead, festival.*

This young Mexican American celebrates the Day of the Dead by wearing face paint and an ornate headdress.

Another important festival honors a more recent battle in Mexican history. In the city of Puebla, southeast of Mexico City, masked dancers perform *La Battalla del Cinco de Mayo*, or The Battle of the Fifth of May. This fiesta celebrates the Mexican army's victory over the French army in 1862. Dancers wear many different types of masks in this fiesta. Some of the masks represent the French troops, some represent the Mexican soldiers, and some represent the local Indians who helped the Mexican soldiers.

In addition to festivals about historical battles, there are masked dances that celebrate Mexican Indian legends passed down from generation to generation. Many of these fiestas include masked dancers who depict both humans and animals.

CHAPTER 12
Disguise and Protection

Camouflage paint helps to hide the faces of soldiers.

Many people use masks to conceal their identity or to make it hard for others to see them. Some people paint masks directly onto their faces. Soldiers often paint their faces before going into battle. If soldiers are in an area with green trees and grass, they paint their faces green. Often they use two shades of green. The dark shade of green is for the higher areas of the face, like the nose and cheeks. The light shade is for the lower areas, like the skin near the eyes. From a distance, the soldier's face will blend with the trees and grass and is difficult to see. This form of disguise is called **camouflage** (KAM uh flahj).

Soldiers wear masks to protect them from harmful gases. Some protective masks are made so soldiers can drink from canteens without removing their masks.

Masks can also provide protection. A common form of protective mask is the gas mask. Gas masks protect people from harmful gases and dust that can hurt or even kill. People working in many different jobs wear gas masks, including soldiers, police officers, and construction workers.

Another type of protective mask is a surgical mask. Doctors and nurses wear surgical masks every time they operate on a patient. Unlike gas masks, surgical masks are not for the protection of the person wearing the mask. Surgical masks protect patients from harmful viruses or bacteria that might be passed on from the breath of the doctors and nurses.

CHAPTER 13
Masks for Fun

Though many people wear masks for serious reasons, some people wear masks just for fun. Masquerade balls have been popular in Europe and America for hundreds of years. People at a masquerade ball wear costumes and masks. Sometimes they dress like historical characters, like pirates or princesses. Other times the costumes and masks are of imaginary creatures, like goblins or fairies. The masked people at the ball talk to others and dance, often without knowing anyone's true identity.

Many people celebrate Mardi Gras by wearing masks or face paint.

At masquerade balls, some people wear masks while they dance and talk.

Another popular occasion for masks in the United States is the October holiday called Halloween. During Halloween, people wear many different kinds of masks. Sometimes the masks are handmade from paper, and sometimes they are plastic masks bought at a store. The masks of Halloween represent almost every different kind of person or creature, both real and imagined. Some masks fit over the entire head, while smaller masks barely cover the eyes. Yet another popular form of masks is made of makeup or face paint.

The holiday Mardi Gras is a popular occasion for wearing face paint. Some Mardi Gras celebrations include contests. People paint their faces and judges choose the winner.

CHAPTER 14
Masks Today

Throughout history people have worn masks, and they still wear them today. People all over the world wear masks for many reasons. Some wear masks in religious rituals, some wear masks for disguise, some wear masks for protection, and some wear masks for fun. Whatever the reason, masks are still as popular today as they were thousands of years ago.

Masks can do many things. Masks let people make believe they are someone else. In an instant a person can put on a mask and pretend to be an animal, a monster, or a popular character from history. Masked dancers teach the history of a group of people by making the past come alive. Making masks, wearing them, or watching others wear them make life more fun and exciting.

Scarecrow masks and costumes are one of many popular disguises during Halloween.

GLOSSARY

amphitheater (AM fuh thee uh tur) – a large outdoor theater used for performing games, contests, or plays.

anthropologist (an thruh PAH luh jist) – a person who studies the origins and development of cultures.

Atamalqualiztli – an ancient Aztec festival where masked dancers swallowed live snakes and frogs.

camouflage (KAM uh flahj) – a disguise that blends with the surrounding environment.

kachina (kuh CHEE nuh) – any of hundreds of spirits or gods believed in by the Hopi and Zuni Indians. Masked dancers act like kachinas during special ceremonies.

kiva (KEE vuh) – a large underground chamber used by Pueblo Indians for religious ceremonies.

pantomime magic (PAN tuh miim MA jik) – a ritual in which tribesmen act out an event to make sure it happens in real life.

shalako (SHAL ah ko) – a large, winter Hopi Indian festival, in which masked dancers perform.

shaman (SHAH mun) – a person who uses magic as a tribal priest or doctor.

tamanawas – a tribal meeting of the Native Americans of the Northwest Coast.

totem pole (TOH tum POHL) – a pole carved and painted by Native Americans of northwest North America.

INDEX